Called to Be Your Song

Prayers for Cantors

MICHAEL E. NOVAK

WORLD LIBRARY PUBLICATIONS
The music and liturgy division of J. S. Paluch Company, Inc.
3708 River Road, Suite 400 • Franklin Park, Illinois 60131-2158
800 566-6150 • www.wlpmusic.com

Called to Be Your Song

WLP 017387
ISBN 978-1-58459-464-2

Author: Michael E. Novak
Editor: Alan J. Hommerding
Copy Editor: Marcia T. Lucey
Typesetting and Design: Denise C. Durand
Director of Publications: Mary Beth Kunde-Anderson
Production Manager: Deb Johnston

Excerpts from the *New American Bible with Revised New Testament and Psalms*, copyright © 1991, 1986, 19770, Confraternity of Christian Doctrine, Inc., Washington, DC. Used with permission. All rights reserved. No part of the *New American Bible* may be reprinted without permission of the copyright holder.

Excerpts from the *New Revised Standard Version Bible*, copyright ©1989, Division of Christian Education of the National Council of the Churches of Christ in the United States of America. Used by permission. All rights reserved.

Excerpts from the English translation of the *Exsultet (Easter Proclamation)* and the English translation of the Introductory Rites for Holy Thursday from *The Roman Missal* © 2010, International Commission on English in the Liturgy Corporation. All rights reserved.

Scripture excerpts from the *Lectionary for Mass for Use in Dioceses of the United States of America* copyright © 1998, 1997, 1970, Confraternity of Christian Doctrine, Inc., Washington, DC. Used with permission. All rights reserved. No part of the *Lectionary for Mass* may be reproduced by any means without permission in writing from the copyright owner.

Second printing

Copyright © 2010, World Library Publications, the music and liturgy division of J. S. Paluch Co., Inc. 3708 River Road, Suite 400, Franklin Park, Illinois 60131-2158. All rights reserved under the United States copyright law. No part of this work may be reproduced or transmitted in any form or format or by any means, whether mechanical, photographic, or electronic, including taping, recording, or photocopying, or any information storage and retrieval systems, without the express written permission of the appropriate copyright holder.

Table of Contents

Dedication 7
A Prayer before Singing 9
Prayers for the Seasons of Grace
Advent
   Preparing for the Lord's Coming 12
   The Lord Has Come 13
   Come into Our Hearts, Lord 14
   The Servant of the Lord 15

Christmas Season
   I Will Not Be Silent 16
   With the Angels 17
   The Word 18
   New Year, New Song 19
   The Light of the Star 20
   Immersed in Song 21

Lent
   Return to the Lord 22
   A Clean Heart 23
   Witness 24
   Living Water 25
   Light of Salvation 26
   Eternal Life 27

Palm Sunday of the Lord's Passion
   Passion and Service 28

The Triduum – Holy Thursday
   Foot Washing 29

The Triduum – Good Friday
    No Greater Love 30

The Triduum – The Easter Vigil
    Alleluia 31

Easter Season
    The Empty Tomb 32
    Seeing and Believing 33
    Our Hearts Burning Within Us 34
    Refreshed by the Shepherd 35
    Praise the Lord 36
    God of All Hopefulness 37
    The Promise of Eternal Life 38

Easter Season – Ascension
    Shout to God 39

Easter Season – Pentecost
    Creator Spirit 40

The Most Holy Trinity
    In Your Likeness 41

The Body and Blood of Christ
    One with Christ 42

Our Lord Jesus Christ the King
    Rejoicing in the House of the Lord 43

Prayers Inspired by the Sunday Psalms
Winter
    Draw Forth Life 46
    I Will Sing Your Praise 47

Summer

Thirsting for God 48
The Bounty of the Lord 49
Ever in My Mouth 50

Autumn

Let Us Bow Down in Worship 51
A Fruitful Harvest 52
The God of Justice 53

Prayers Before Sacraments, Special Occasions, and Other Celebrations

Before a Baptism 56
Before a Celebration of Confirmation 57
Before a Celebration of First Communion 58
Before a Reconciliation Service 59
Before a Celebration of Anointing of the Sick 60
Before a Wedding 61
Before a Celebration of Holy Orders 62
Before a Funeral 63
Before a Celebration of Sunday Eucharist 64
Before Morning Prayer 65
Before Evening Prayer 66
Preparing for a Major Event 67
Before Celebrating with a Small Assembly 68
Before an Early Liturgy 69
Before Celebrating a Liturgy of the Word 70
Before a Liturgy with Children 71
Before an Ecumenical Service 72
Before an Interfaith Service 73
Thanksgiving Day 74

The Life and Ministry of a Cantor

Thanksgiving for the Gift of Song 76
First Time Singing as a Cantor 77
Beginning to Prepare Music for a Liturgy 78
Learning a New Song 79
Preparing Challenging Music 80
Preparing Music I Don't Like 81
Preparing Music in an Unfamiliar Language 82
When Drafted as a Last-minute Substitute 83
When Singing as a Substitute in a
   Different Community 84
In a New Parish or Community 85
When I Have a Sore Throat 86
Running Late 87
Stuck in Traffic on the Way 88
When I've Been Too Busy to Prepare 89
Facing Imperfections 90
Praying the Psalms 92
Before Singing a Lament 94
When Distracted by Worries and Cares 95
When Cantors Gather 96
Thanksgiving After Liturgy 97

Scripture Index 98

Dedication

For Judy,
whose love always keeps me focused on God's song.

A Prayer before Singing

O God,
help me to proclaim your presence
to your holy people.

Amen.

Prayers for the Seasons of Grace

Advent

Preparing for the Lord's Coming

He will keep you firm to the end, irreproachable on the day of our Lord Jesus Christ.

1 Corinthians 1:8

God of all time,
seldom are we more mindful
of the fleet passage of time
than during these short, dark days
before the winter solstice.

Help me to seek you
as we enter into
this great season of Advent,
our time of longing for the light.

Teach me to sing a song
that will rouse the hearts of your people
and make them ready for your coming.

May our worship and our lives
help to bring the world closer to that glorious day,
for you live and reign for ever and ever.

Amen.

Advent

The Lord Has Come

Shout with exultation, O city of Zion,
for great in your midst
is the Holy One of Israel!

Isaiah 12:6

In the midst of our Advent preparations, O God,
we know that you have already
come into the world.
Heaven and earth have exulted;
your reign has been proclaimed.

We have already rejoiced,
we continue to rejoice,
and we prepare to rejoice even more.

Let me lift up my voice
to sing and shout with joy.
Let all the people hear it—
the Holy One has come!

May we joyfully raise our voices,
singing praise to you
who live for ever and ever.

Amen.

Advent

Come into Our Hearts, Lord

O Lord of hosts, restore us;
Let your face shine upon us,
that we may be saved.

Psalm 80:4

O loving God,
you know my innermost thoughts
and my deepest longings.

As I recall your coming into human history
and await your glorious return,
I implore you
to come into my heart this Christmas.

Fill me with your love,
that more and more
my life will be given to your service.
May everything I do,
every song I sing,
lead others closer to you.

O come, O come, Emmanuel!

Amen.

Advent

The Servant of the Lord

"Behold, I am the handmaid of the Lord. May it be done to me according to your word."

Luke 1:38

O God of our salvation,
because she knew your song by heart,
the Virgin Mary
accepted your invitation
to carry your Son into the world.

Fill me with your song;
    let it overflow my being
    so that I can do no other
    than to bring you eagerly
    to all my brothers and sisters.

May the song we sing together
    rattle the rafters
    and shake the world
    with the sound of your goodness
    for ever and ever.

Amen.

Christmas Season

I Will Not Be Silent

For Zion's sake I will not be silent,
for Jerusalem's sake I will not be quiet.

Isaiah 62:1

God of love,
in the stillness of the night,
in a little tiny baby,
you spanned the chasm
between heaven and earth.

How could anyone be silent
in the face of such a marvel?
On this holy night
together with the angels
and all of creation
we rejoice with heart and soul and voice.

May the joyful Christmas song
in which I am blessed to take a part
spill over
into a joyful Christmas life
that proclaims your coming
in all that I do.

Amen.

Christmas Season

With the Angels

And suddenly there was a multitude of the heavenly host with the angel, praising God.

Luke 2:13

God of hosts,
    at the birth of your Son Jesus
    all of heaven burst out
in a mighty song to your glory.

We who walked in darkness
    have seen the great light of salvation
    in his holy face.

Help us all to express
    our profound joy and gratitude
    through the words, rhythms, and melodies
    of the music we will sing today,
    that we may all join with the angels
    in their holy song of praise.

Amen.

Christmas Season

The Word

And the Word became flesh
and made his dwelling among us.

John 1:14

God of infinite expressiveness,
your Son is called the Word,
for he is the very expression
of your infinite love and goodness.

We say and sing words every day,
   words that animate,
   words that injure,
   words whose full meaning we fail to grasp.

Fill our words of worship today
   with light and life.
Grant that the words of joy and hope
   that we sing on this bright Christmas day—
   and that I am blessed to proclaim—
   will come to life
   the rest of the year
   in everything we do.

Amen.

Christmas Season

New Year, New Song

In times past, God spoke in partial and various ways to our ancestors through the prophets; in these last days, [God] spoke to us through a son.

Hebrews 1:1–2

O God of new beginnings,
as a new year begins,
many speak of "turning over a new leaf."

If it's possible, I pray to "turn over a new song."
Mary did it
    when she sang your praise in the Magnificat.
The shepherds did it
    when they returned glorifying and praising you.

Give my life a new tune today,
    a new meter to march to,
    a new key to unlock the wonders of your creation
    and live as one of your creatures
    praising you night and day,
    for you are indeed Lord of all
    for ever and ever.

Amen.

Christmas Season

The Light of the Star

And behold, the star that they had seen at its rising preceded them, until it came and stopped over the place where the child was.

Matthew 2:9

O God of wonder and might,
    you used a star
    to show seekers the way to your Son.

At times it can be a challenge,
    in the midst of my enthusiasm
    for the music,
    to keep from drawing attention
    to myself and my singing.

Teach me the lesson of the star of Bethlehem,
    that my task is not to be the way
    but to show the way,
    so that your pilgrim people may come and adore.

May I always offer my gift
    in a spirit of true humility
    to you who are Lord
    for ever and ever.

Amen.

Christmas Season

Immersed in Song

On coming up out of the water he saw the heavens being torn open and the Spirit, like a dove, descending upon him.

Mark 1:10

O God of infinite variety,
you showed yourself to us in your Son,
and you continue to show yourself to us
in all of your marvelous creation.

Your people stand at the banks of your river of song.
Help me to immerse them in your praise
 so that they may know the presence of your Spirit
 and renew their baptismal call
 to be pleasing in your sight
 and a light for the nations.

May we become even more
 a people through whom
 you continue to show yourself
 to the world.

Amen.

Lent

Return to the Lord

Even now, says the LORD,
 return to me with your whole heart,
 with fasting, and weeping, and mourning;
Rend your hearts, not your garments,
 and return to the LORD, your God.

Joel 2:12–13

God of mercy and compassion,
now is an acceptable time
to return to you with all my heart.

As the sober song of this Lenten season begins,
 may I remember that it is also
 a season of joy,
 for we are always your people
 and you are always our God.

Give me a renewed heart this Lent;
 may my sincere efforts
 to change my life
 bring me and your penitent people
 to a new alleluia this Easter.

Amen.

Lent

A Clean Heart

A clean heart create for me, O God;
and a steadfast spirit renew within me.

Psalm 51:12

God of the wilderness,
your Son knew the desert sands
and I know the desert of the soul.

Sometimes when I sing your song,
my heart is not in it—
not because I don't believe the words,
but because of an empty yearning
that seems to grow out of everyday life.

My soul wanders into the desert
and the only path out
is marked by the words of your song.

Give me the grace
to sing through my yearning,
to make that my song,
so that your people may know
an authentic witness to your mercy.

O Lord, open my lips,
and my mouth shall proclaim your praise.

Amen.

Lent

Witness

Bear your share of hardship for the gospel with the strength that comes from God.

2 Timothy 1:8

Life-giving God,
you sustain those who
continue the mission of Jesus your Son.

In the midst of my preparations
 of music and verse,
 help me to know and embrace
 the mission that you have for me.

May my willingness to do your will
 be reflected in the way
 that I lead the prayer of your gathered people,
 so that bit by bit
 our community of believers
 will be transformed
 into the likeness of Jesus your Son,
 who lives and reigns for ever and ever.

Amen.

Lent

Living Water

"[W]hoever drinks the water I shall give will never thirst; the water I shall give will become in [them] a spring of water welling up to eternal life."

John 4:14

O God, Source of all that is good,
you are the wellspring
of life within us.

Serving you and your beloved people in the liturgy
can be fulfilling,
but it is also demanding.
Every celebration calls forth from me
finer musical skills
and greater spiritual depth.

Cultivate in me a thirst for improvement;
encourage me to hone my musical skills,
and invite me to become more familiar with you
in the holy scriptures
and in the people whom you have called me to
serve.

May your life-giving waters
well up within me
as a sign of your eternal faithfulness
to all your people,
who know salvation
in Jesus Christ our Lord.

Amen.

Lent

Light of Salvation

Live as children of light, for light produces every kind of goodness and righteousness and truth.

Ephesians 5:8–9

God of light,
the hours of daylight are lengthening
and our Lenten spring is halfway over.

We rejoice in your presence
   even as we continue our Lenten penitence,
   for we know that the glimmer of light
   we see now is but a pale gleam
   compared to the brilliance of Easter.

Sharpen in me an awareness
   of the bad habits into which I have fallen
   as a musician and leader of prayer,
   so that I may refresh my ministry
   as well as my life of faith
   during this Lenten season of renewal.

May the light of your grace
   grow brighter in me
   as a sign of the eternal light
   that you offer to all of us
   through Jesus Christ our Lord.

Amen.

Lent

Eternal Life

Then you shall know that I am the Lord, when I open your graves and have you rise from them, O my people!

Ezekiel 37:13

O God of life,
you revel in the abundance
of all that springs up from the earth
and flourishes anew
in the radiance of your presence.

Bring forth in me
 a new resolve to serve you;
 remove the shackles
 that keep me from becoming
 everything that I can be
 for you and your people.

Stir up in me a fresh desire
 to spread your Good News
 to all the world.

May the new life of your love
 grow within me
 as a sign of the salvation won for all of us
 in Jesus Christ,
 who is the resurrection and the life.

Amen.

Palm Sunday of the Lord's Passion

Passion and Service

*The Lord G<small>OD</small> has given me
   a well-trained tongue,
that I might know how to speak to the weary
   a word that will rouse them.*

Isaiah 50:4

Merciful God,
the passion of your Son Jesus Christ
reminds us of the sufferings
of many in this world.

We who remember today
   the height of Jesus' triumphal entry into Jerusalem
   and the depth of his trial and crucifixion
   need also recall that we rise with him
   in his glorious resurrection
   and assume his ministry to the lowly of the world.

May we who lead the celebration today
   work to keep all who gather here in worship
   mindful of this call to service
   that they have received
   through their baptism
   into the passion and resurrection
   of your Son, our Lord Jesus Christ,
   who lives with you for ever and ever.

Amen.

The Triduum – Holy Thursday

Foot Washing

We should glory in the cross of our Lord Jesus Christ, for he is our salvation, our life and our resurrection; through him we are saved and made free.

Introductory Rites for Holy Thursday

Loving God,
your only Son gave himself,
Body and Blood,
for our salvation.

As I prepare for this celebration
    of the opening liturgy
    of the sacred Triduum,
    call forth in me
    the attitude of Jesus at the Last Supper.

May the service that I perform
    be a musical foot-washing for your people.

Foster in me
    the manner of a servant
    as a sign to your people
    of the service that we are called to render
    to all in your holy name,
    for you are Lord for ever and ever.

Amen.

The Triduum – Good Friday

No Greater Love

Who would believe what we have heard?
  To whom has the arm of the Lord been revealed?

Isaiah 53:1

Passionate God,
  your only Son gave himself
  to be nailed to a tree
for our sakes.

As I prepare for this celebration,
  help me to be aware
  of the responsibility that I have
  to sing the story of your love
  so that all will believe
  more deeply, more truly.

Make me a conduit of your grace,
  that your people assembled here
  will see, not me,
  but your holy cross and passion
  that they, too, may bear witness
  to your great love.

I make this prayer in Jesus' name,
  our Lord and Savior.

Amen.

The Triduum – The Easter Vigil

Alleluia

Rejoice, heavenly powers! Sing, choirs of angels!
   Exult, all creation around God's throne!
   Jesus Christ, our King, is risen!
   Sound the trumpet of salvation!

Exsultet

O Lord of life,
   your only Son
   rose from the dead
and lives forever in glory with you.

As I prepare for this holiest of nights,
   make me an alleluia for your people.
Fill my voice, my posture, my gestures
   with ineffable joy
   at the glorious resurrection
   of Jesus Christ, your Son.

Allow me to be the trumpet
   that sounds salvation for all your people,
   so that they may rejoice
   and go forth to share the news
   that Christ is risen
   and death reigns no more.

Amen. Alleluia!

Easter Season

The Empty Tomb

[T]hey did not yet understand the Scripture that he had to rise from the dead.

John 20:9

Transforming God,
   you have made an empty tomb
   a sign of ultimate fulfillment.
I cannot begin to imagine
   the miracles you can work in me.

On this holiest of days
   keep me focused on the message
   of the joyful songs that I sing.
Help our music to stir up
   in the hearts of your people
   the question of what it means
   to rise from the dead.
May they find the answer in you.

May the acoustics of the empty tomb
   make a perfect reverberation
   of our songs of praise.

Amen. Alleluia!

Easter Season

Seeing and Believing

Although you have not seen him you love him; even though you do not see him now yet believe in him, you rejoice with an indescribable and glorious joy.

1 Peter 1:8

O God of the possible,
you raise up faith in you
in the hearts of all who seek you.

Your faithful people have never seen you,
   and yet we know you,
   for, paradoxically, we have seen you.
We have seen you in the sunrise,
   we have seen you in the quiet stream,
   we have seen you in the mighty storm.
But most of all, we have seen you
   in the faces of those in need.

Bless my music this day.
May our community see in my ministry
   the risen Jesus Christ,
   and so praise you
   and go forth
   ready to do your will.

Amen. Alleluia!

Easter Season

Our Hearts Burning Within Us

"Were not our hearts burning within us while he spoke to us on the way and opened the scriptures to us?"

Luke 24:32

Resourceful God,
   you are always seeking new ways
   to come into our hearts
through the things we know in this world.

Make my heart burn within me today
   that I may be for your people
   a sacrament of your presence
   that leads them to know you
   in the breaking of the bread.

As they recognize you,
   may their hearts, too,
   burn with your presence,
   so that when we all leave
   the table of your love
   we will share your Good News
   with all the world,
   through Christ Jesus our Lord.

Amen. Alleluia!

Easter Season

Refreshed by the Shepherd

The LORD is my shepherd; I shall not want.
 In verdant pastures he gives me repose;
beside restful waters he leads me
 he refreshes my soul.

Psalm 23:1–3

O Divine Shepherd,
you guide me in your ways
and refresh me by the waters of your love.

At this point in the Easter season,
 all my initial energy has been spent.
Lilies have wilted and
 alleluias have become common.

Good Shepherd,
 refresh my singing;
 lead me to new insights in the texts
 and new delight in the melodies.
Put a new spring in the rhythms
 and a revitalized pulse in the meters.

May your Easter people
 see your new song in me
 and respond Alleluia
 with a new-found joy.

Amen. Alleluia!

Easter Season

Praise the Lord

*Exult, you just, in the L*ORD*;*
  praise from the upright is fitting.
*Give thanks to the L*ORD *on the harp;*
  with the ten-stringed lyre chant his praises.

Psalm 33:1–2

Almighty God,
you have no need of our praise
and yet we can do no other.

Fill me with your praise today;
  may the songs in which
  I lead your people
  ring out with beauty and power
  and the goodness of you.

As your people sing with me,
  may we together make our lives
  a continuous hymn
  to the glory of your name,
  through Christ our risen Lord.

Amen. Alleluia!

Easter Season

God of All Hopefulness

Always be ready to give an explanation to anyone who asks you for a reason for your hope.

1 Peter 3:15

God of hope,
no matter our situation
you always give us good reason
to hope in you.

Whenever I sing at a liturgy,
    I always come from
    whatever is happening in my life.
Sometimes I have more hope than others.

Be with me today,
    in my song and in my life,
    and fill me with hope
    in the new life and resurrection
    that are given to all of us
    in Christ Jesus your Son.

As I sing today,
    may your holy people
    also see the hope that you give
    and rejoice anew in your love
    through Christ our risen Lord.

Amen. Alleluia!

Easter Season

The Promise of Eternal Life

*I believe that I shall enjoy the Lord's goodness
    in the land of the living.*

Psalm 27:13

God of the living,
   your blessed Son
   redeemed us so that we would be able
to live with him forever in the land of the living.

As we near the end of this Easter season,
   renew in my heart
   faith in your promise of eternal life
   for those who love you.

May those who hear my voice
   hear your promise as well,
   and so renew their Easter joy
   in our risen savior,
   Jesus Christ,
   who is Lord for ever and ever.

Amen. Alleluia!

Easter Season – Ascension

Shout to God

All you peoples, clap your hands,
shout to God with cries of gladness,
*for the L*ord*, the Most High, the awesome,*
is the great king over all the earth.

Psalm 47:2–3

Almighty God,
your Son has gone up with a shout,
to trumpet blasts is he enthroned.

There are times when I am timid in my ministry,
when my gestures are hesitant,
when my voice is small.

Teach me to extol you
with shouts of joy,
with clapping when the Spirit moves,
that I may praise you exuberantly.

When I am able to lead your people
with such energy,
may their praise catch fire
and raise the roof
to your glory,
for ever and ever.

Amen. Alleluia!

Easter Season – Pentecost
Creator Spirit

If you take away their breath, they perish
   and return to their dust.
When you send forth your spirit, they are created.

Psalm 104:29–30

Creator God,
   you have made everything in its goodness,
   and given life and breath through your Spirit.

Send your Holy Spirit upon me,
   inspire me with your love and light.
When I breathe,
   support my song with your strong creative wind.
When I move,
   light my gestures with the gift of your fire.

May all who are gathered here see in me
   the inspiration of your Spirit,
   and be moved to renew the face of the earth
   in the name of Jesus Christ your Son
   and in the Spirit of all that is holy.

Amen. Alleluia!

The Most Holy Trinity

In Your Likeness

The grace of the Lord Jesus Christ
and the love of God
and the fellowship of the Holy Spirit be with all of you.
2 Corinthians 13:13

O most holy God,
Father all-powerful,
Jesus Christ, Lord and Savior,
Spirit of love,
you made us in your likeness.

As we celebrate the mystery of your Trinity,
help me to be a sign of your grace
in the way that I communicate
your saving message.
Help me to be a sign of your love
in the way that I dedicate myself to your ministry.
Help me to be a sign of your fellowship
in the way that I am present to your people.

May we who gather here today
take your grace and love and fellowship
with us into the world in your name,
for you are one God
for ever and ever.

Amen.

The Body and Blood of Christ

One with Christ

Because the loaf of bread is one, we, though many, are one body, for we all partake of the one loaf.

1 Corinthians 10:17

Lord Jesus Christ,
>   you commanded us to remember you
>   in the breaking of the bread
and the sharing of the cup.

As I prepare for worship today,
>   remind me of what a privilege it is
>   to share your Body and Blood
>   and so become one with you.

May the song that I offer
>   and the life that I live
>   be a fitting thanksgiving
>   for the salvation you have won
>   for all of us.

Grant that I may one day live with you in the kingdom
>   where you live for ever and ever.

Amen.

Our Lord Jesus Christ the King

Rejoicing in the House of the Lord

I rejoiced because they said to me,
   "We will go up to the house of the LORD."

Psalm 122:1

Almighty and merciful God,
   by the death and resurrection of your Son,
   our Lord Jesus Christ, King of all creation,
we are redeemed and made whole.

As I prepare for today's celebration,
   fill me anew with joy
   at the redemption that Christ the King
   has won for us,
   so that I will be ready
   to lead your faithful people, rejoicing,
   into your holy presence.

May the joy that we feel today be contagious
   as we go forth to invite our neighbors and friends
   to the house of the Lord,
   who rules in glory
   for ever and ever.

Amen.

Prayers Inspired by the Sunday Psalms

The Sunday Psalms of Winter

Draw Forth Life

Your ways, O Lord, make known to me;
    teach me your paths,
guide me in your truth and teach me,
    for you are God my savior.

Psalm 25:4–5

O God of wisdom,
    even in the dark and cold of winter,
    you draw forth life from creation.

Teach me your ways,
    and draw forth from me
    the very best that I can offer
    in my music and in my prayer.

When I lead your faithful people in worship,
    draw forth from them, too,
    the best that they have to offer,
    so that they may praise you with their lives
    through Jesus Christ, our Lord.

Amen.

The Sunday Psalms of Winter

I Will Sing Your Praise

[I]n the presence of the angels I will sing your praise;
I will worship at your holy temple
and give thanks to your name.

Psalm 138:1–2

At times, O Lord my God,
it is good to do nothing
but give you praise.

I always seem to be on the move,
running from one activity to the next,
preparing this, rehearsing that.
Of course, it is important to practice.

But when the time for the prayer comes, O Lord,
teach me to stop running and just be.
Let me just be in your presence.
Let me just be the melody,
the words, the rhythm.
Let me just be the conduit of your love,
singing your song in the presence of the angels.
Then your chosen people will know
that you are there,
and they, too, will sing in the presence of the angels.

Blessed be your name for ever and ever.

Amen.

The Sunday Psalms of Summer

Thirsting for God

O God, you are my God whom I seek;
for you my flesh pines and my soul thirsts
like the earth, parched, lifeless and without water.

Psalm 63:2

Sometimes I cannot sense your presence, O Lord.
I know that you are there, waiting for me,
but all I see is the cracked, dusty earth.

At those times, the psalms I sing
   can be a lifeline back to you.
Even when I feel nothing inside,
   just singing the words is a comfort
   that lets me know I am not forgotten.

Be with me, Lord, in those dry times,
   so that the words of praise I sing
   in the midst of the assembly
   are not empty husks
   but filled with your love for your people.

Grant this prayer through Christ, our Lord,
   who came to quench our thirst for your presence.
Amen.

The Sunday Psalms of Summer

The Bounty of the Lord

The eyes of all look hopefully to you,
*   and you give them their food in due season;*
you open your hand
*   and satisfy the desire of every living thing.*

Psalm 145:15–16

O God of life,
    you fill the earth with abundance
    to feed every living thing.
As summer proceeds,
    the lushness and lavishness of your bounty
    are ever more evident.

Inspire in me an attitude of gratefulness
    for the bounty of summertime.
May this gratitude find expression
    in the way I sing your psalms
    and lead the prayer of your faithful people.

When they hear me, may they, too,
    be thankful for your generosity,
    and so turn with generous hearts
    to their neighbors in need,
    through Christ our Lord
    who gave abundantly of himself
    for the salvation of the world.

Amen.

The Sunday Psalms of Summer

Ever in My Mouth

I will bless the Lord at all times;
   [God's] praise shall be ever in my mouth.
Let my soul glory in the Lord;
   the lowly will hear me and be glad.

Psalm 34:2–3

Great are you, Lord God,
and worthy
of all praise!

It sometimes seems a tall order
   to have your praise ever in my mouth, O God.
There are distractions, frustrations,
   and injustices that tug and pull
   and capture my attention.
Help me to see all these things in my life
   through the lens of your attentive care
   and the love that you gave to us
   in the person of your only Son.

Bit by bit, fill me with your praise,
   so that your chosen people,
   especially the lowly,
   will indeed hear me and be glad.

Praise and honor be yours
   for ever and ever.

Amen.

The Sunday Psalms of Autumn

Let Us Bow Down in Worship

Come, let us sing joyfully to the Lord;
  let us acclaim the Rock of our salvation.
Come, let us bow down in worship;
  let us kneel before the Lord who made us.

Psalm 95:1, 6

Almighty God,
  all blessings flow from you
  and we praise you for your wonderful works.

As a minister of the liturgy,
  I bear some responsibility
  for how the community enters into our worship.
Help me to foster an attitude
  of prayerfulness and devotion
  by my bearing and posture
  as well as through my singing and movement.

Foster in me a humble heart
  so that when I bow down in worship,
  your assembled people will feel invited
  to kneel before you who made us.

May our entire liturgy be
  one song of thankfulness and praise
  as we acclaim you, the rock of our salvation,
  now and forever.

Amen.

The Sunday Psalms of Autumn

A Fruitful Harvest

Blessed are you who fear the Lord,
*   who walk in [God's] ways!*
For you shall eat the fruit of your handiwork;
*   blessed shall you be, and favored.*

Psalm 128:1–2

O God of the harvest,
plentiful and abundant are the crops
that you have given us to cultivate.

During this autumn time,
    make me mindful not only of the harvest of food,
    but also of the harvest of souls.
Give me the insight to see
    how my ministry of music and word
    is also a ministry of evangelization.
Help me to capture in tune and rhythm and word
    the invitation that you extend
    to all who come inside our welcoming walls.

May my attitude be that of Christ,
    who walked perfectly in your ways,
    starting a harvest that continues to this day
    and will extend to the end of time.

Amen.

The Sunday Psalms of Autumn

The God of Justice

The LORD keeps faith forever,
 secures justice for the oppressed,
 gives food to the hungry.
The LORD sets captives free.

Psalm 146:6–7

O God of justice,
you rule the world with righteousness
and call us all to account for our actions.

Make me mindful, O Lord,
 of the implications of the words that I sing,
 for you desire not only sacrifice,
 but acts of justice and right.
Give me a righteous heart
 and a desire to serve your lowly ones,
 so that when I sing of your justice,
 the words of my mouth may be
 consonant with the actions of my life.

When your holy people hear me,
 they will know of the power of your word
 and work more diligently with you
 to bring about your kingdom
 through our Lord Jesus Christ,
 in whose name we faithfully gather.

Amen.

Before Sacraments, Special Occasions, and Other Celebrations

Before a Baptism

[A]ll of you who were baptized into Christ have clothed yourselves with Christ.

Gracious Galatians 3:27

Gracious God,
   at your invitation we are baptized
   into the death and resurrection of
Christ Jesus, your Son.

Preparing for this celebration,
   help me to be mindful of my own baptism
   and the many graces of that day
   that have touched and directed my life.
Filled with these recollections,
   may I sing today's songs
   with deeper conviction
   and more profound joy.

May those who celebrate this sacrament today
   depart with the sure knowledge
   that they are clothed with Christ,
   whose name they now bear,
   and who is Lord for ever and ever.

Amen.

Before a Celebration of Confirmation

[T]he love of God has been poured out into our hearts through the holy Spirit that has been given to us.

Romans 5:5

O God of power and might,
    through your Holy Spirit
    you continue to enliven the hearts
of your faithful.

As I prepare for this celebration,
    fill me with the gifts of the Spirit.
May the melodies that I sing and
    the words to which I give voice
    be imbued with the fire of your love.

May those who participate in this celebration
    witness the powerful work of the Spirit
    in the lives of the confirmation candidates
    and praise you for all your wonderful works.

Bless us all with the inspiration of your Spirit
    for the spreading of your Good News
    and for the good of all the world.

Grant this prayer through Jesus Christ,
    who lives and reigns with you
    and that same Holy Spirit,
    one God for ever and ever.

Amen.

Before a Celebration of First Communion

"I am the bread of life; whoever comes to me will never hunger, and whoever believes in me will never thirst."

John 6:35

Nourishing God,
you feed us with the Bread of Life
in your Son, Jesus Christ our Lord.

As I prepare for this celebration,
   call to my mind my own First Communion.
How eager I was to participate
   in your holy banquet!
May I bring to my music today
   some of that ardent anticipation of your presence,
   a reminder that every time we share the Eucharist
   is a privilege and a blessing.

May those who celebrate today
   embark on a lifetime of sharing
   the Body and Blood
   of Jesus Christ our Lord,
   who gave himself as our food
   for our salvation.

Amen.

Before a Reconciliation Service

[T]he Lamb who is in the center of the throne will shepherd them and lead them to springs of life-giving water.

Revelation 7:17

O Lamb of God
who takes away the sins of the world,
you know my heart in its depths,
my weaknesses and my sinfulness.

Fill me today with your gracious spirit
of reconciliation
that I may share it in song
with my brothers and sisters
who have gathered in that reconciling spirit.

May the songs that we sing today
unite us in your love
and bring us to new life,
for you are our merciful Lord
for ever and ever.

Amen.

Before a Celebration of Anointing of the Sick

Are any among you sick? They should call for the elders of the church and have them pray over them, anointing them with oil in the name of the Lord.

James 5:14 (NRSV)

Healing God,
you transformed your Son's
suffering on the cross
into victory and life.

As I prepare for this celebration,
may I be mindful of human frailties
and the suffering caused by injury and disease,
so that I may be responsive to the needs
of those who have come today
for this sacrament.
Instill in me also
confidence in your healing presence,
that your people may continue to hope in you
and your merciful love.
Comfort and fortify them
through the music that I am privileged
to lead them in singing.

May all who gather here today
be filled with the strength of the Holy Spirit
and ready to embrace your will
through Jesus Christ our Lord.

Amen.

Before a Wedding

[I]f we love one another, God remains in us, and [God's] love is brought to perfection in us.

1 John 4:12

O God of love,
you are the author
of every human desire for unity
with one another.

As I prepare for this wedding,
    keep me mindful of the sacrament of love
    that will unfold in the midst of this community.

Give me the poise
    to invite participation graciously,
    the grace
    to provide musical leadership joyfully,
    and the generosity of spirit
    to praise you lavishly
    at this great celebration of your
    infinite love.

I make this prayer
    through Jesus Christ,
    who enriched the wedding celebration at Cana
    and fills all our lives
    with your boundless love
    for ever and ever.

Amen.

Before a Celebration of Holy Orders

As each one has receive a gift, use it to serve one another as good stewards of God's varied grace.

1 Peter 4:10

Gracious God,
you have chosen each of us
to serve you and your people
according to the gifts you have given us.

As I prepare for this celebration,
may I be mindful of the many gifts
that you have bestowed on our community.
On this happy day,
fill me with joy that these workers in your vineyard
are receiving your grace and blessing
to carry on the mission of Jesus Christ
together with your faithful people.

May our song of gratitude resound among the rafters
as we pray that the good work
begun by you in these your servants
may be brought to fulfillment
through Jesus Christ our Lord.

Amen.

Before a Funeral

*[T]he souls of the just are in the hand of God
and no torment shall touch them.*

Wisdom 3:1

O God of mercy and compassion,
through your Son's death and resurrection,
you have overcome death for us.

As I prepare for this liturgy,
  imbue me with your compassion,
    that I may be sensitive to the needs and feelings
    of your people on this occasion.
Fill me with gratitude for your Son's resurrection,
  that my faith in your salvation
  may be evident in how I sing and pray.

May your people know the comfort that comes
  from the sure knowledge
  of your mercy and love,
  and have confidence in the redemption won
  by Jesus Christ, who is Lord of life
  for ever and ever.

Amen.

Before a Sunday Eucharist

[B]ring me to your holy mountain,
*   to the place of your dwelling,*
That I may come to the altar of God,
*   to God, my joy, my delight.*

Psalm 43:3–4

Almighty God,
I am blessed
to serve your people
through your gift of music.

Be with me and in me today
as I proclaim your word
and sing your song
in this celebration of the Eucharist.

May we all sing your praises
both here and with you in heaven
for ever and ever.

Amen.

Before Morning Prayer

*It is good to give thanks to the L*ORD*,*
 to sing praise to your name, Most High,
To proclaim your love in the morning.

Psalm 92:2–3

God of darkness and dawn,
you have given us the gift
of another day.

It is good to praise your name
in the morning,
before the busy-ness of the day sets in.

Let us warm up our voices and our hearts
so that we may live today
conscious of your gift of life
and your love for us.

May the psalms and prayers that I proclaim
give your people hope and strength
for the challenges that this day will bring,
and may we depart
renewed in our zeal to do your will,
through Christ our Lord.

Amen.

Before Evening Prayer

"Stay with us, for it is nearly evening and the day is almost over."

Luke 24:29

God of dawn and darkness,
we have lived through
your gift of another day.

It is good to praise your name
in the evening,
to thank you for all that has been
and look forward to a night of repose in your grace.

Let us raise our day-weary voices and our hearts
so that we may reflect
on the deeds of this day
and your love for us.

May the psalms and prayers that I proclaim
give your people comfort and perspective
as they ponder today's events,
conscious of your presence throughout the day.
May we depart
refreshed in heart and soul,
confident of your mercy and forgiveness,
through Christ our Lord.

Amen.

Preparing for a Major Event

*Let everything that has breath
    give praise to the L{\scriptsize ORD}!
Hallelujah!*

Psalm 150:6

Gracious God,
because of the gift of music you have given me
I have been asked to be the cantor
at this celebration of _____.

Help me to prepare well,
   to know the music and my part in it thoroughly.
Calm my nerves and my fears with your presence;
   grant me poise to move and sing gracefully,
   and presence of mind to deal with the unexpected.

May I be transparent to your presence
   so that those in attendance will hear your voice
   in my ministry.

Should some see fit to praise me afterward,
   may I be gracious in acknowledging your gift
   and quick to thank you for your good grace.

Praise and thanks be to you, O God,
   for ever and ever.

Amen.

Before Celebrating with a Small Assembly

"[W]here two or three are gathered together in my name, there am I in the midst of them."

Matthew 18:20

O God of the greatest and the least,
you are found
wherever your name is invoked.

Today a small group is gathered
in your name.

Be with me in my ministry to them,
and help me to acknowledge your presence
in this gathering
as much as I do in a full church.
Bring me to a deep appreciation
of the intimate quality of your company
that can be found in such groups
and so to adapt
the way that I sing and lead
accordingly.

May I bless your name
wherever you are found
for ever and ever.
Amen.

Before an Early Liturgy

Very early when the sun had risen, on the first day of the week, they came to the tomb.

Mark 16:2

O God of all of time,
we know your presence
in every hour of the day,
and have learned that your greatest works
come before the dawn.

As I prepare for this early liturgy,
    may I warm up my voice with your praises,
    and awaken my heart knowing of your love.

When your faithful people arrive,
    help me to get them ready to pray.
May my ministry arouse their spirits
    and give them reason to acknowledge
    your gift of a new day
    that we may dedicate to you
    through Jesus Christ our Lord.

Amen.

Before Celebrating a Liturgy of the Word

Your word is a lamp for my feet,
a light for my path.

Psalm 119:105

O God of infinite love,
your Word became flesh and blood
and lived among us.

As I prepare to celebrate this Liturgy of the Word,
may I keep in mind
the power of your holy word.
Let the tunes and rhythms of the music
not obscure the meaning of the text
but bring it to life.
Let my diction carry every syllable
to the ears of your assembled people.

When we listen to and pray your word together,
O Lord,
may it enlighten us
and light our path through the world,
through Jesus Christ our Lord.

Amen.

Before a Liturgy with Children

Jesus said, "Let the children come to me, and do not prevent them; for the kingdom of heaven belongs to such as these."

Matthew 19:14

God of love,
your love for your people
is revealed especially in the children.

As I prepare for this celebration,
give me the heart of a child,
that I may approach you
with eagerness and wonder,
ready to hear your word
and respond with sincerity.

Give me a new appreciation
for the children's depth of feeling
and richness of experience,
for they are the present of the Church,
and not just its future.

May my ministry to them make your love
tangible and infectious,
and may I be open to the grace
that they bring to this prayer,
through Jesus Christ,
who is Lord for ever and ever.

Amen.

Before an Ecumenical Service

[There is] one Lord, one faith, one baptism; one God and Father of all, who is over all and through all and in all.

Ephesians 4:5–6

God of all,
    in you we find our common faith,
    our unity.

Though our communities of faith are separate,
    we are united by our baptism
    and our desire to become
    ever more closely united in Christ.

As I prepare to celebrate
    with my brothers and sisters in Christ,
    may our common music be a sign
    of Jesus' prayer that we all may be one.

May the things that still separate us
    inspire us to work with renewed fervor
    to remove every last obstacle
    so that we all may celebrate
    complete unity in Christ
    for ever and ever.

Amen.

Before an Interfaith Service

[M]y house shall be called
a house of prayer for all peoples.

Isaiah 56:7

God of the nations,
even though we come
from many faith traditions,
you unite all your people in a bond of love.

As I prepare to celebrate
with my brothers and sisters of many faiths,
give me a heart that is open and welcoming
to the grand diversity of your goodness.
May our common music be a sign
that your grace overcomes all divisions.

Grant that we who unite in your praise
may also unite in proclaiming
your steadfast love to all the world.

Amen.

Thanksgiving Day

And now, bless the God of all,
   who has done wondrous things on earth.

Sirach 50:22

O God of the harvest,
every good thing we have
comes from your hand.

As I prepare for this celebration,
   fill me with gratitude
   for the good things of the earth,
   for your bountiful love,
   and for the gift of eternal life
   won for us by your Son, Jesus Christ.

In the songs that I lead today,
   may your grateful people bless you
   and praise you
   and thank you
   with their entire being,
   for you are our great and glorious
   God for ever and ever.

Amen.

The Life and Ministry of a Cantor

Thanksgiving for the Gift of Song

Sing to the L<small>ORD</small> a new song;
sing to the L<small>ORD</small>, all the earth.

Psalm 96:1

O God who created the music
of the heavenly spheres,
you have blessed me with the gift of song.

From my earliest days I have carried a tune,
marched to a meter,
danced a rhythm that welled up inside me.

Your gift of music has given me joy,
has given me a language to express
my deepest longings,
my crushing heartbreaks.

In return for this gift, O God,
I offer it back to you
with a grateful heart.
May I use it in the midst of the assembly
to sing your praise,
to lament with the brokenhearted,
and to raise a voice for the voiceless
that they may be heard in your name.

Grant this prayer through Jesus Christ, your Son,
your Word and your Song,
who reigns with you for ever and ever.

Amen.

First Time Singing as a Cantor

Sing to the LORD a new song
a hymn in the assembly of the faithful.

Psalm 149:1

Lord, you have called me and I have answered.
I cannot keep your song
bottled up within me.

I ask you today to be with me
and in me
all through this liturgy,
as I humbly offer to you and your people
the gift of music with which I have been blessed.

May your people hear in my voice
your holy presence,
and may my musical prayer
bring them closer to you.

Keep me ever mindful of the great privilege it is
to sing your praises in the midst of the assembly.
Help me to grow in your love
every time I sing,
and may I never stop learning
new and better ways
to lead your people's praise
of your holy name.

Amen.

Beginning to Prepare Music for a Liturgy

*When the builders had laid the foundation of the L*ORD*'s temple, the vested priests with the trumpets and the Levites, sons of Asaph, were stationed there with the cymbals to praise the L*ORD *in the manner laid down by David, king of Israel.*

Ezra 3:10

O God who delights in all beauty,
you have blessed me
with this opportunity
to lead the sung prayer
of your Spirit-filled people.

Give me the perseverance
to practice and learn this music well.
Enlighten my mind to the meaning of these words.
Teach my lips to sing these your praises
and fill my heart with your presence.

May I bring this music before our community
in a spirit of humility and prayerfulness
to the greater glory of your name.

Amen.

Learning a New Song

*In the beginning was the Word,
and the Word was with God,
and the Word was God.*

John 1:1

O God of all beginnings,
you have set before me
this gift of new music
that will be used to praise your name
in the midst of the assembly.

Give me a sharp eye to read the notes well,
and a discerning ear to perfect their tones.
May I detect in the rhythms
the movements of your presence.

Grant me an understanding heart,
that I may make the words my own
and learn to use them
to proclaim your presence to your people
with expressiveness and passion.

May this song become through me
an instrument of your beauty and truth,
in Jesus' name.

Amen.

Preparing Challenging Music

*Mountains and hills shall break out in song before you,
    and all the trees of the countryside shall clap their hands.*

Isaiah 55:12

O God of infinite variety,
in your wisdom you have made it possible
for us to create songs that are simple
and also music that is complex and challenging.

As I work through this piece of music,
    help me to find you
    in the intricacies of its rhythms
    and the leaps of its melodies.

Bit by bit,
    as I learn the geography of this song,
    its hills and valleys,
    may I come to love your presence here
    and make it a part of my being.

When I sing this song,
    may all who hear it
    come to love your presence here, too.

Amen.

Preparing Music I Don't Like

"We played the flute for you, but you did not dance, we sang a dirge but you did not mourn."

Matthew 11:17

O patient God,
   I don't always get to choose
   the music that I am to sing
or lead for liturgy.
Sometimes the music chosen
   is not to my taste.

Teach me, O Lord,
   that your holy Church is made up
   of many members,
   that the song that may leave one cold
   moves another to tears.
You speak to your people in many ways
   and perhaps the scope of my judgment
   needs to be broader.

When I am preparing music that I don't like,
   help me to learn its language
   and express your meaning in it,
   so that when I sing it
   your prayerful people hear only your voice
   calling them to you.

I make this prayer in the name of
   Christ Jesus, your Son,
   who is Lord for ever and ever.

Amen.

Preparing Music in an Unfamiliar Language

"[W]e hear them speaking in our own tongues of the mighty acts of God."
Acts 2:11

God of every nation,
   all peoples of the world
   rightly give you thanks and praise,
each in their own tongue.

I have been asked to prepare song
   in a language with which I am unfamiliar.
There will be those at this celebration
   for whom hearing this tongue
   will be a blessing, a comfort, and an inspiration.
Teach me the words and accents that I need to know;
   give me the humility to seek the help that I need,
   and the confidence to know that
   my careful preparation will carry me through.

When your assembled people hear these words,
   may they bless you for the gift of diversity
   that you have bestowed upon your Church,
   and rejoice in the richness of your creation.

Praise and thanks to you
   for the manifold gifts of the Spirit
   given to your Church for the good of the world.

Amen.

When Drafted as a Last-minute Substitute

Then I heard the voice of the Lord saying, "Whom shall I send? Who will go for us?" "Here I am;" I said; "send me!"

Isaiah 6:8

O God of surprises,
    when I woke up this morning,
    little did I know the task in store for me.
By your grace,
   someone has enough confidence
   in the musical gifts you have given me
   to ask me at the last minute
   to fill in as cantor.

Help me to see that,
   even though I have not been able
   to practice for this liturgy,
   every moment that I have spent in practice
   for other occasions
   has enabled me to prepare for this one.

Give me the grace to offer my efforts today
   in an attitude of prayer and humility.
Grant me the poise of the Holy Spirit,
   that your presence may be seen
   and your praise be heard
   in all that I do.

Amen.

When Singing as a Substitute in a Different Community

[T]he Lord appointed seventy-two others whom he sent ahead of him in pairs to every town and place he intended to visit.

Luke 10:1

O God of pilgrims,
    you have called me today
    to lead the sung prayer of your people
in a community with which I am unfamiliar.

As I prepare to sing,
    help me to remember that your Word
    and your presence
    are ever the same.

Let me see your face in those of the people here,
    and as I minister to them in song,
    may they hear your voice in mine,
    to the glory of your name
    for ever and ever.

Amen.

In a New Parish or Community

*But how could we sing a song of the Lord
   in a foreign land?*

Psalm 137:4

O God of new beginnings,
you have led me
to another place
where your praises are sung.

The faces in the pews are different;
   help me to come to love them.
The networks and supports are unfamiliar;
   acclimate me to them.
The music is not what I'm accustomed to;
   familiarize me with its melodies and rhythms.

Even as I remember my old spiritual home
   with fondness,
   fill me with anticipation
   for all the wonderful new ways
   that I will experience you
   in your people
   and in my ministry.

Together let us sing a new song
   to your glory.

Amen.

When I Have a Sore Throat

"My grace is sufficient for you, for power is made perfect in weakness."
2 Corinthians 12:9

O God, source of health and life,
today I am barely able to speak,
let alone sing.
Yet I must be ready to lead your faithful people
in the sung prayers of this liturgy.

Give my voice the stamina and strength it needs
to make it through this celebration.
May I have the creativity to delegate and rearrange
when possible,
and the discipline not to abuse my vocal cords,
but to allow you to be heard
in my "tiny whispering sound."

When this liturgy is over,
grant me a speedy return
to good health
and vocal vigor.

Amen.

Running Late

"[O]f that day and hour no one knows, neither the angels of heaven, nor the Son, but the Father alone."

Matthew 24:36

O God of all time,
you fill every moment with your presence
and give us the precious gift of time.

Somehow I have let the hours of the day
> get away from me,
> and now I am rushing
> to make myself ready
> and get to church on time.

Fill me with calm and quiet
> that when I arrive
> I may approach the liturgy
> with poise and prayerfulness
> and the attentiveness
> that your baptized people deserve.

When the liturgy is done,
> deepen in me
> a respect for your presence
> in your holy people
> so that I will be a better steward of my time
> in preparing to celebrate with them.

May I always find ways
> to make time for you, O God,
> through Jesus Christ our Lord.

Amen.

Stuck in Traffic on the Way

Remember how for forty years now the LORD, your God, has directed all your journeying in the desert, so as to test you by affliction.

Deuteronomy 8:2

O God of inscrutable ways,
  I left in plenty of time to get to church,
  but it appears that you have other plans for me.

Give me patience and a spirit of courtesy on the road,
  that I may approach with good humor
  a situation that I cannot change.

Give me a resourceful attitude and presence of mind,
  so that I can find ways
  to communicate my situation
  with those who need to know
  and perhaps uncover an alternate route
  to speed my arrival.

Give me a light heart,
  so that when I do arrive at my destination
  I may focus on the task at hand
  and be ready to lead your people in song
  with a renewed sense of perspective and purpose.

May this adventure remind me
  that all of my life is subject
  to your loving direction.

Amen.

When I've Been Too Busy to Prepare

*There is an appointed time for everything
    and a time for every affair under the heavens.*

Ecclesiastes 3:1

O God of time,
    I have let time slip away
    and now I feel under-prepared for this liturgy.

Forgive my procrastination
    and my forgetfulness.

By your grace,
    carry me through my responsibilities today;
    calm me when my nerves threaten to undo me,
    and pick me up when I stumble
    so that your people may sing your praises
        anyway.

And please gently remind me
    of the priorities that I must set
    in order to carry out
    the ministry that has been entrusted to me
    in your holy name.

Amen.

Facing Imperfection

*The fear of the LORD is training for wisdom,
and humility goes before honors.*

Proverbs 15:33

Patient and merciful God,
in your wisdom you have made us humans
fallible and imperfect.

When I lose the tune,
sing the wrong words,
miss an entrance,
or make any of a thousand mistakes,
my humanity shows all too clearly.

Despite all my preparation
something went wrong today.
Did your people notice?
Maybe.
Probably not.
Even so, you were still praised.

Grant me the grace to accept my imperfections,
and the humility to acknowledge
that I will stumble even on the best of days.
Help me to remember
that with all my warts,
I am still your instrument,
called to minister to your faithful people.

To you be all glory and praise
through Jesus Christ your Son
for ever and ever.

Amen.

Praying the Psalms

*Praise the L*ORD*, my soul;*
*I shall praise the L*ORD *all my life,*
sing praise to my God while I live.

Psalm 146:2

Gracious God,
whom saints and angels
delight to worship in heaven,
you have given to cantors
the special charism of proclaiming the psalms
in the midst of your assembly.
I am privileged to have been called
to this holy ministry.

Cultivate in me a deep and abiding love
for your word in the scriptures,
especially for the sacred psalms.
Give me an inquiring mind,
that I may seek to enrich my knowledge
of their meaning
through research and study.
Teach me to pray the psalms frequently
as an expression of my faith in you.

Most of all,
nurture in me a profound devotion
to your chosen people,
whose every sentiment and emotion
finds expression in these sublime songs to you.

May I grow ever closer to you
 in this ministry of song
 with which I have been blessed,
 through Jesus Christ,
 who is your Son and Song
 throughout all eternity.

Amen.

Before Singing a Lament

How long, Lord? Will you utterly forget me?
  How long will you hide your face from me?

Psalm 13:2

Sometimes, O God, when things seem hopeless,
it is difficult to sing your praises.
Yet we still must pray and sing to you,
so we sing lamentations
and cry out to you in our pain.

When I sing psalms and canticles of lament,
  help me to bring to them
  my times of doubt,
  my experiences of desolation,
  so that your suffering people will know
  an authentic voice expressing their cries of pain.
Even in our suffering, O Lord,
  help us to find your presence,
  for our very crying out to you
  is an acknowledgment of your
  compassion and grace.

We know that you listen to our prayers, O Lord,
  whatever form they take,
  for you are our merciful and loving God
  from of old
  and for evermore to come.

Amen.

When Distracted by Worries and Cares

"Martha, Martha, you are anxious and worried about many things. There is need of only one thing."

Luke 10:41–42

O faithful God,
   you know the prayers of our hearts
   even when they are confused and distracted.

Sometimes when I am scheduled to cantor,
   my mind is far away,
      on other matters that distract and worry me.

When this happens,
   gently call me back to the task at hand.
Help me to focus on the needs and prayers
   of the faithful who are in front of me.
Teach me to unite my concerns
   with the prayer of your holy people,
   so that your name is praised
   with my full attention and skill.

Praise and honor be yours, merciful God,
   through Jesus Christ our Lord.

Amen.

When Cantors Gather

On that day David ... appointed the singing of praises to the Lord by Asaph and his kindred ...
Blessed be the Lord, the God of Israel,
*   from everlasting to everlasting."*

1 Chronicles 16:7, 36 (NRSV)

Creator God,
>   you have blessed humanity
>   with the gift of music,
and endowed us with the ability
to sing your praises in numerous ways.

Bless our gathering here today;
>   fill our work and prayer and song
>   with your presence and power.
May our efforts today bear fruit
>   to the glory of your name
>   in the midst of the faithful.

Bless each of us in our ministry
>   that we may continue to bring your people
>   closer to you in the songs that we sing
>   and the lives that we lead.

Praise and thanksgiving to you, O God,
>   through Jesus Christ our Lord.

Amen.

Thanksgiving After Liturgy

*Sing to the Lord, all the earth,
announce his salvation, day after day.*

1 Chronicles 16:23

O bountiful God,
you are the source
of every good gift.

You have blessed me
with the gift of song
to praise your name with beauty and grace.
Thank you for the opportunity today
to lead your faithful people
in singing to your holy name.

Grant that our musical prayer together
will move us to serve others
and continue to live the mission
given us by Jesus Christ, who is Lord
for ever and ever.

Amen.

Scripture Index

Deuteronomy 8:2	*Life & Ministry of a Cantor:* Stuck in Traffic on the Way, 88
Ezra 3:10	*Life & Ministry of a Cantor:* Beginning to Prepare Music for a Liturgy, 78
1 Chronicles 16:7, 36 (NRSV)	*Life & Ministry of a Cantor:* When Cantors Gather, 96
1 Chronicles 16:23	*Life & Ministry of a Cantor:* Thanksgiving After Liturgy, 97
Psalm 13:2	*Life & Ministry of a Cantor:* Before Singing a Lament, 94
Psalm 23:1–3	*Easter Season:* Refreshed by the Shepherd, 35
Psalm 25:4–5	*The Sunday Psalms of Winter:* Draw Forth Life, 46
Psalm 27:13	*Easter Season:* The Promise of Eternal Life, 38
Psalm 33:1–2	*Easter Season:* Praise the Lord, 36
Psalm 34:2–3	*The Sunday Psalms of Summer:* Ever in My Mouth, 50
Psalm 43:3–4	*Sacraments and Special Occasions:* Before a Sunday Eucharist, 64
Psalm 47:2–3	*Easter Season – Ascension:* Shout to God, 39
Psalm 51:12	*Lent:* A Clean Heart, 23
Psalm 63:2	*The Sunday Psalms of Summer:* Thirsting for God, 48
Psalm 80:4	*Advent:* Come into Our Hearts, Lord, 14
Psalm 92:2–3	*Sacraments & Special Occasions:* Before Morning Prayer, 65

Psalm 95:1, 6	*The Sunday Psalms of Autumn:* Let Us Bow Down in Worship, 51
Psalm 96:1	*Life & Ministry of a Cantor:* Thanksgiving for the Gift of Song, 76
Psalm 104:29–30	*Easter Season – Pentecost:* Creator Spirit, 40
Psalm 119:105	*Sacraments & Special Occasions:* Before Celebrating a Liturgy of the Word, 70
Psalm 122:1	*Our Lord Jesus Christ the King:* Rejoicing in the House of the Lord, 43
Psalm 128:1–2	*The Sunday Psalms of Autumn:* A Fruitful Harvest, 52
Psalm 137:4	*Life & Ministry of a Cantor:* In a New Parish or Community, 85
Psalm 138:1–2	*The Sunday Psalms of Winter:* I Will Sing Your Praise, 47
Psalm 145:15–16	*The Sunday Psalms of Summer:* The Bounty of the Lord, 49
Psalm 146:2	*Life & Ministry of a Cantor:* Praying the Psalms, 92
Psalm 146:6–7	*The Sunday Psalms of Autumn:* The God of Justice, 53
Psalm 149:1	*Life & Ministry of a Cantor:* First Time Singing as a Cantor, 77
Psalm 150:6	*Sacraments & Special Occasions:* Preparing for a Major Event, 67
Proverbs 15:33	*Life & Ministry of a Cantor:* Facing Imperfection, 90
Ecclesiastes 3:1	*Life & Ministry of a Cantor:* When I've Been Too Busy to Prepare, 89

Wisdom 3:1	*Sacraments & Special Occasions:* Before a Funeral, 63
Sirach 50:22	*Sacraments & Special Occasions:* Thanksgiving Day, 74
Isaiah 6:8	*Life & Ministry of a Cantor:* When Drafted as a Last-minute Substitute, 83
Isaiah 12:6	*Advent:* The Lord Has Come, 13
Isaiah 50:4	*Palm Sunday:* Passion and Service, 28
Isaiah 53:1	*The Triduum – Good Friday:* No Greater Love, 30
Isaiah 55:12	*Life & Ministry of a Cantor:* Preparing Challenging Music, 80
Isaiah 56:7	*Sacraments & Special Occasions:* Before an Interfaith Service, 73
Isaiah 62:1	*Christmas Season:* I Will Not Be Silent, 16
Ezekiel 37:13	*Lent:* Eternal Life, 27
Joel 2:12–13	*Lent:* Return to the Lord, 22
Matthew 2:9	*Christmas Season:* The Light of the Star, 20
Matthew 11:17	*Life & Ministry of a Cantor:* Preparing Music I Don't Like, 81
Matthew 18:20	*Sacraments & Special Occasions:* Before Celebrating with a Small Assembly, 68
Matthew 19:14	*Sacraments & Special Occasions:* Before a Liturgy with Children, 71
Matthew 24:36	*Life & Ministry of a Cantor:* Running Late, 87

Mark 1:10	*Christmas Season:* Immersed in Song, 21
Mark 16:2	*Sacraments & Special Occasions:* Before an Early Liturgy, 69
Luke 1:38	*Advent:* The Servant of the Lord, 15
Luke 2:13	*Christmas Season:* With the Angels, 17
Luke 10:1	*Life & Ministry of a Cantor:* When Singing as a Substitute in a Different Community, 84
Luke 10:41–42	*Life & Ministry of a Cantor:* When Distracted by Worries and Cares, 95
Luke 24:29	*Sacraments & Special Occasions:* Before Evening Prayer, 66
Luke 24:32	*Easter Season:* Our Hearts Burning Within Us, 34
John 1:1	*Life & Ministry of a Cantor:* Learning a New Song, 79
John 1:14	*Christmas Season:* The Word, 18
John 4:14	*Lent:* Living Water, 25
John 6:35	*Sacraments & Special Occasions:* Before a Celebration of First Communion, 58
John 20:9	*Easter Season:* The Empty Tomb, 32
Acts 2:11	*Life & Ministry of a Cantor:* Preparing Music in an Unfamiliar Language, 82
Romans 5:5	*Sacraments & Special Occasions:* Before a Celebration of Confirmation, 57
1 Corinthians 1:8	*Advent:* Preparing for the Lord's Coming, 12

1 Corinthians 10:17	*The Body and Blood of Christ:* One with Christ, 42
2 Corinthians 12:9	*Life & Ministry of a Cantor:* When I Have a Sore Throat, 86
2 Corinthians 13:13	*The Most Holy Trinity:* In Your Likeness, 41
Galatians 3:27	*Sacraments & Special Occasions:* Before a Baptism, 56
Ephesians 4:5–6	*Sacraments & Special Occasions:* Before an Ecumenical Service, 72
Ephesians 5:8–9	*Lent:* Light of Salvation, 26
2 Timothy 1:8	*Lent:* Witness, 24
Hebrews 1:2–2	*Christmas Season:* New Year, New Song, 19
James 5:14 (NRSV)	*Sacraments & Special Occasions:* Before a Celebration of Anointing of the Sick, 60
1 Peter 1:8	*Easter Season:* Seeing and Believing, 33
1 Peter 3:15	*Easter Season:* God of All Hopefulness, 37
1 Peter 4:10	*Sacraments & Special Occasions:* Before a Celebration of Holy Orders, 62
1 John 4:12	*Sacraments & Special Occasions:* Before a Wedding, 61
Revelation 7:17	*Sacraments & Special Occasions:* Before a Reconciliation Service, 59

Michael E. Novak

Michael E. Novak holds degrees in theology from Georgetown University in Washington, D.C., and Spring Hill College in Mobile, Alabama. He works as Parish Resources Editor at World Library Publications, where he is responsible for the annual book of Sunday scripture reflections, *Living the Word*, as well as numerous resources produced to assist parishes with their Sunday bulletins and other publications. He edited the art/meditation books *In Shining Splendor* and *Canticle*, and served as managing editor for *Preach* magazine.

A cantor for over thirty years, Mike is a former director of the Office for Prayer and Worship for the Archdiocese of Milwaukee. He is presently a cantor at the Cathedral of Saint John the Evangelist in Milwaukee, where he also directs the Men's Choir. With years of parish and campus ministry experience, he writes and presents talks and workshops on liturgy, music, the catechumenate, liturgical design, and the sacraments. He is a past member of the national board of directors of the Federation of Diocesan Liturgical Commissions, and has taught Christian initiation as adjunct faculty at St. Francis Seminary in Milwaukee, Wisconsin. Articles that he authored have appeared in *Ministry and Liturgy, Catechumenate, AIM*, and *Prayer & Worship*.